MY RV
A USER'S GUIDE

By P. McCallum
Edited by P. Lind

Cover Art by Fred Broussard

Digitally produced by:

CONVERPAGE
23 Acorn Street
Scituate, MA 02066   ISBN: 0-9728155-5-4
781-378-1996   Copyright 2006

PREFACE

It's funny, I never camped when I was growing up.   Not that I've grown up yet but in this "later" stage of childhood I've camped in the back of a pickup, tent camped (in a fancy two-room tent), advanced to a pop-up trailer, then a travel trailer, then a Class C, and now a Class A, I guess my next move would be a Class E or F??, whatever that may be, I'll certainly look into it.

As part of my camping experience, my family and friends have included fishing, boating, canoeing, golf, bike riding, clamming, dog walking, dog hiking, dogs around the campfire. There are at least 2-3 dogs on every camping trip. It certainly keeps it cozy on those 90 degree nights, especially when my 119 lb (not 120, he's sensitive about his weight) yellow lab, Bailey decides to snuggle up at night after a day on the clam flats.

Part of the enjoyment of RV'ing is planning our trips, maintaining the RV, packing up and keeping important records.

MY RV helps us keep all of our information together - from checklists to keeping track of maintenance to keeping track of friends we meet on the road. Have a safe trip!

CONTENTS

PART I - CHECKLISTS

CONTENTS (Cont'd)

Part II - RV Log

CONTENTS (Cont'd)

... 115
... 123
Camp Inspection ... 125

... 170

Part II —

Introduction ... 141
Carried out ... 155
Camp preparations ... 213
Recipes ... 243
Important Addresses and Numbers ... 276
The Sponsors ... 303
Notes ... 333

PART I - CHECKLISTS

MY RV

This section allows you to record all the information about your RV including owner information, insurance, registration, etc.

Being prepared with all this information and having it right at your fingertips is one of the many benefits you will find in this guide! Fill in your dealer information or can attach the sales and service department's business cards on the sheet. You should also include all of the Manufacturer's information as you may be traveling anywhere in the U.S. and this information will be very useful in the event of needed repairs or maintenance.

OWNER INFORMATION

Names _____

Address _____

City _____ State _____ Zip Code _____

Phone Number _____ _____

Cell Phone Number _____ _____

Insurance Company _____

Policy Number _____

Insurance Agent_____

Address _____

Phone No. _____

RV Registration # _____

MY RV

Year_____Make_____

Model_____

VIN# _____

Purchase Date_____

Dealer Name_____

Street Address_____

City/State/Zip_____

Sales Person _____

Email_____

Dealer Website_____

Sales Phone No._____

Service Phone No. _____

Cell No. _____

<u>MY RV</u> (Cont'd)

YOU CAN ATTACH SALES & SERVICE DEPT.
BUSINESS CARDS TO THE BACK OF THIS SHEET
AS WELL

Manufacturer Information:

_____

_____

_____

_____

WARRANTY INFORMATION

It's important to go through your Owner's Manual and walk through your RV making a list of items throughout the RV from appliances to major parts. Note the serial #, model # and warranty time period. If anything should go wrong, all of your information is together. You can also contact the RV manufacturer and request electrical and plumbing schematics, which can be very useful.

WARRANTY INFORMATION

Description _____

Model#_____Serial#_____

Warranty Period_____

Manufacturer_____

Address _____

_____

Phone#_____

Description _____

Model#_____Serial#_____

Warranty Period_____

Manufacturer_____

Address _____

_____

Phone#_____

WARRANTY INFORMATION

Description _____

Model#_____Serial#_____

Warranty Period_____

Manufacturer_____

Address _____

_____

Phone#_____

Description _____

Model#_____Serial#_____

Warranty Period_____

Manufacturer_____

Address _____

_____

Phone#_____

WARRANTY INFORMATION

Description _____

Model#_____Serial#_____

Warranty Period_____

Manufacturer_____

Address _____

_____

Phone#_____

Description _____

Model#_____Serial#_____

Warranty Period_____

Manufacturer_____

Address _____

_____

Phone#_____

WARRANTY INFORMATION

Description _____

Model#_____Serial#_____

Warranty Period_____

Manufacturer_____

Address _____

_____

Phone#_____

Description _____

Model#_____Serial#_____

Warranty Period_____

Manufacturer_____

Address _____

_____

Phone#_____

WARRANTY INFORMATION

Description _____

Model#_____Serial#_____

Warranty Period_____

Manufacturer_____

Address _____

_____

Phone#_____

Description _____

Model#_____Serial#_____

Warranty Period_____

Manufacturer_____

Address _____

_____

Phone#_____

WARRANTY INFORMATION

Description _____

Model#_____Serial#_____

Warranty Period_____

Manufacturer_____

Address _____

_____

Phone#_____

Description _____

Model#_____Serial#_____

Warranty Period_____

Manufacturer_____

Address _____

_____

Phone#_____

WARRANTY INFORMATION

Description _____

Model#_____Serial#_____

Warranty Period_____

Manufacturer_____

Address _____

_____

Phone#_____

Description _____

Model#_____Serial#_____

Warranty Period_____

Manufacturer_____

Address _____

_____

Phone#_____

WARRANTY INFORMATION

Description _____

Model#_____Serial#_____

Warranty Period_____

Manufacturer_____

Address _____

_____

Phone#_____

Description _____

Model#_____Serial#_____

Warranty Period_____

Manufacturer_____

Address _____

_____

Phone#_____

WARRANTY INFORMATION

Description _____

Model#_____Serial#_____

Warranty Period_____

Manufacturer_____

Address _____

_____

Phone#_____

Description _____

Model#_____Serial#_____

Warranty Period_____

Manufacturer_____

Address _____

_____

Phone#_____

EMERGENCY INFORMATION

If an emergency should occur while on the road, this section can be the most crucial. Providing family contacts, current medical conditions, medications, allergies and physician information are so important during the first response to an emergency. This information can make such a difference in the outcome. We mention family members, but make a point to include all guests, especially children.

Keep all of this information together and carry copies with you if you're in a separate travel vehicle sightseeing or out for the day. They won't help if they are stored back at the RV...

Let's remember too, camping is a fun enjoyable experience for everyone. Many campsites can be in secluded areas and even if they're not, there is that possibility that you or someone in your group could get into a dangerous situation with a person or even an animal. Using some safety precautions may help protect campers from these unexpected situations.

FAMILY CONTACTS

Family Member/Guest_____

Address _____

_____

D.O.B. _____

Phone Nos. _____ _____

Medical Information

Existing Family Medical Conditions (medications, current illnesses, allergies):

_____

_____

_____

Physician Name:_____

Address: _____

_____

Phone No. _____

FAMILY MEMBER (Cont'd)

(Name – Cont'd) _____

Insurance Company: _____

_____

Member No._____

Phone No. _____

Notes _____

_____

Contact Person _____

(Relation)_____

Address _____

_____

Phone No. _____

Phone No. (cell) _____

Email Address _____

FAMILY CONTACTS

Family Member/Guest_____

Address _____

_____

D.O.B.   _____

Phone Nos. _____ _____

Medical Information

Existing Family Medical Conditions (medications, current illnesses, allergies):

_____

_____

_____

Physician Name:_____

Address: _____

_____

Phone No. _____

FAMILY MEMBER (Cont'd)

(Name – Cont'd) _____

Insurance Company: _____

_____

Member No._____

Phone No. _____

Notes _____

_____

Contact Person _____

(Relation)_____

Address _____

_____

Phone No. _____

Phone No. (cell) _____

Email Address _____

FAMILY CONTACTS

Family Member/Guest_____

Address _____

_____

D.O.B. _____

Phone Nos. _____   _____

Medical Information

Existing Family Medical Conditions (medications, current illnesses, allergies):

_____

_____

_____

Physician Name:_____

Address: _____

_____

Phone No. _____

FAMILY MEMBER (Cont'd)

(Name – Cont'd) _____

Insurance Company: _____

_____

Member No._____

Phone No. _____

Notes _____

_____

Contact Person _____

(Relation)_____

Address _____

_____

Phone No. _____

Phone No. (cell) _____

Email Address _____

FAMILY CONTACTS

Family Member/Guest_____

Address _____

_____

D.O.B.   _____

Phone Nos. _____   _____

Medical Information

Existing Family Medical Conditions (medications, current illnesses, allergies):

_____

_____

_____

Physician Name:_____

Address: _____

_____

Phone No. _____

FAMILY MEMBER (Cont'd)

(Name – Cont'd) _____

Insurance Company: _____

_____

Member No._____

Phone No. _____

Notes _____

_____

Contact Person _____

(Relation)_____

Address _____

_____

Phone No. _____

Phone No. (cell) _____

Email Address _____

FAMILY CONTACTS

Family Member/Guest_____

Address _____

_____

D.O.B. _____

Phone Nos. _____ _____

Medical Information

Existing Family Medical Conditions (medications, current illnesses, allergies):

_____

_____

_____

Physician Name:_____

Address: _____

_____

Phone No. _____

FAMILY MEMBER (Cont'd)

(Name - Cont'd) _____

Insurance Company: _____

_____

Member No. _____

Phone No. _____

Notes _____

_____

Contact Person _____

(Relation) _____

Address _____

_____

Phone No. _____

Phone No. (cell) _____

Email Address _____

FAMILY CONTACTS

Family Member/Guest_____

Address _____

_____

D.O.B. _____

Phone Nos. _____ _____

Medical Information

Existing Family Medical Conditions (medications, current illnesses, allergies):

_____

_____

_____

Physician Name:_____

Address: _____

_____

Phone No. _____

FAMILY MEMBER (Cont'd)

(Name - Cont'd) _____

Insurance Company: _____

_____

Member No._____

Phone No. _____

Notes _____

_____

Contact Person _____

(Relation)_____

Address _____

_____

Phone No. _____

Phone No. (cell) _____

Email Address _____

FAMILY CONTACTS

Family Member/Guest_____

 Address _____

 _____

D.O.B.   _____

Phone Nos. _____   _____

Medical Information

Existing Family Medical Conditions (medications, current illnesses, allergies):

_____

_____

_____

 Physician Name:_____

 Address: _____

 _____

 Phone No. _____

FAMILY MEMBER (Cont'd)

(Name - Cont'd) _____

Insurance Company: _____

_____

Member No._____

Phone No. _____

Notes _____

_____

Contact Person _____

(Relation)_____

Address _____

_____

Phone No. _____

Phone No. (cell) _____

Email Address _____

FAMILY CONTACTS

Family Member/Guest_____

Address _____

_____

D.O.B. _____

Phone Nos. _____ _____

Medical Information

Existing Family Medical Conditions (medications, current illnesses, allergies):

_____

_____

_____

Physician Name:_____

Address: _____

_____

Phone No. _____

FAMILY MEMBER (Cont'd)

(Name – Cont'd) _____

Insurance Company: _____

_____

Member No._____

Phone No. _____

Notes _____

_____

Contact Person _____

(Relation)_____

Address _____

_____

Phone No. _____

Phone No. (cell) _____

Email Address _____

FAMILY CONTACTS

Family Member/Guest_____

Address _____

_____

D.O.B. _____

Phone Nos. _____ _____

Medical Information

<u>Existing Family Medical Conditions (medications, current illnesses, allergies):</u>

_____

_____

_____

Physician Name:_____

Address: _____

_____

Phone No. _____

FAMILY MEMBER (Cont'd)

(Name – Cont'd) _____

Insurance Company: _____

_____

Member No._____

Phone No. _____

Notes _____

_____

Contact Person _____

(Relation)_____

Address _____

_____

Phone No. _____

Phone No. (cell) _____

Email Address _____

PET MEDICAL INFORMATION

Oh yes! **Don't forget your pets too!** Medication and Veterinarian information. Your vet may need to be contacted in the event of an illness or injury to your pet.

Make a note of your pets' feeding schedule and amounts in case someone has to care for your pet during an emergency

If you travel with your pet consider having an ID Chip surgically implanted. This is a simple procedure and is a permanent identifier if your pet is lost anywhere in the country. Talk to your vet about this procedure.

PET EMERGENCY INFORMATION

Pet Name _____

Breed_____

Age _____

Veterinarian

Veterinarian Name _____

Address _____

_____

Phone No. _____

Pet Medications _____

_____

Medication Info (Dosage, how often, etc.) _____

_____

Allergies _____

_____

PET EMERGENCY (Cont'd)

Rabies Certificate _____ Attach a copy to this form

License # _____

Pet ID Implant: _____

Feeding: Brand and Amount of Food _____

_____

_____

A.M. _____   P.M. _____

Notes _____

_____

_____

_____

_____

_____

PET EMERGENCY INFORMATION

Pet Name _____

Breed_____

Age _____

Veterinarian

Veterinarian Name _____

Address _____

_____

Phone No. _____

Pet Medications _____

_____

Medication Info (Dosage, how often, etc.) _____

_____

Allergies _____

_____

PET EMERGENCY (Cont'd)

Rabies Certificate _____ Attach a copy to this form

License # _____

Pet ID Implant: _____

Feeding: Brand and Amount of Food _____

_____

_____

A.M. _____   P.M. _____

Notes _____

_____

_____

_____

_____

_____

PET EMERGENCY INFORMATION

Pet Name _____

Breed_____

Age _____

Veterinarian

Veterinarian Name _____

Address _____

_____

Phone No. _____

Pet Medications _____

_____

Medication Info (Dosage, how often, etc.) _____

_____

Allergies _____

_____

PET EMERGENCY (Cont'd)

Rabies Certificate _____ Attach a copy to this form

License # _____

Pet ID Implant: _____

Feeding: Brand and Amount of Food _____

_____

_____

A.M. _____   P.M. _____

Notes _____

_____

_____

_____

_____

PET EMERGENCY INFORMATION

Pet Name _____

Breed_____

Age _____

Veterinarian

Veterinarian Name _____

Address _____

_____

Phone No. _____

Pet Medications _____

_____

Medication Info (Dosage, how often, etc.) _____

_____

Allergies _____

_____

PET EMERGENCY (Cont'd)

Rabies Certificate _____ Attach a copy to this form

License # _____

Pet ID Implant: _____

Feeding: Brand and Amount of Food _____

_____

_____

A.M. _____   P.M. _____

Notes _____

_____

_____

_____

_____

_____

SAFETY TIPS

* Consider installing an alarm system in your RV

* A good pair of walkie talkies for all parties, especially the kids, to stay in contact around the campground or from tent to RV overnight. If you're on a hike and a party gets lost make sure they have access to communication items.

* A GPS

* A cell phone (make sure it's fully charged at all times)

* Purchase plenty of outdoor lights for around your campsite

* Make sure all kids have been educated as far as talking to strangers. There's so much literature in schools and from your town's Safety Officer. Have them learn the information and make a game by quizzing them while during the ride. A good idea for the adults too. Never walk alone. Make sure you're always with a buddy.

* Check smoke detectors and CO_2 detectors in camper.

* Check each states local laws as far as carrying handguns, weapons, mace, etc. There are very strict laws that vary from state to state. Your trip could come to an abrupt end if you are carrying a firearm illegally into a state where you're unfamiliar with the laws.

ARRIVAL & DEPARTURE CHECKLISTS

O.K. folks! We've talked about the technical serious stuff, now let's get down to the real meat and potatoes. We sit in the house during the winter talking and planning our camping trips. Pull out the calendar and start scheduling, start ordering things we must have this coming season to make our time in the wilderness or on the roadways pleasant and comfortable. Don't ruin or delay your trip by forgetting a quick simple procedure. Sometimes all the excitement overshadows the many important tasks that must be done to make your trip safe and enjoyable.

Note: The Departure list consists of specific tasks that should be done when departing from a campground. At the end of the list you will notice we have provided additional procedures for departing from home base.

ARRIVAL LIST

☐ When arriving at campsite - get out of vehicle and check site - location of hookups, fireplace, Back in or drive straight in, etc.

☐ Allow room for slide outs if needed.

☐ Bring camper into site.

☐ Place chock blocks under tires and blocks under leveling jacks.

☐ Unhook trailer from hitch and secure.

☐ Turn on propane tanks.

☐ Connect electricity - make sure breaker is on

☐ Connect water hose and turn on water

☐ Connect sewer hose securely (if full hookup)

☐ Connect cable TV connection if available

☐ Bring slides out if available

ARRIVAL LIST (Cont'd)

☐ Run hot water to fill water heater tank and turn on water heater

☐ Turn refrigerator on to run on AC

☐ Check toilet chemicals

☐ Bring awning out

☐ Bring all outside items out - carpet, grilles, chairs, tables

☐ If traveling with pets, bring out fresh water bowls, food bowls, leashes, runs and toys

☐ Unpack all items inside

☐ Introduce yourself to neighbors. Do they need any help setting up? You may need help sometime!

☐ **Lastly**, make a point to keep in contact with family and friends when arriving so they know all is well and you are safe

ARRIVAL LIST

☐ _____

☐ _____

☐ _____

☐ _____

☐ _____

☐ _____

☐ _____

☐ _____

☐ _____

DEPARTURE LIST

INSIDE

☐ Secure all loose items, coffee makers, cups dishes, bath items etc.

☐ **Secure** TV(s)

☐ **Lower** roof antenna (hang ignition or door keys on crank to remind you)

☐ Close skylights

☐ Bring in slide room

☐ Turn off water pump

☐ Turn off water heater

☐ Close all cabinets and make sure items are secure

☐ Unplug electrical items

☐ Close windows and blinds

☐ Close bathroom, bedroom & shower doors

DEPARTURE LIST (Cont'd)

☐ Turn off A/C and heater

☐ Secure items in refrigerator

☐ Secure cutting boards, sink items, range cover

OUTSIDE

☐ Bring in awning

☐ Pack away all outside items: chairs, carpets, grilles, tablecloths

☐ Lift or remove stabilizing jacks and pack away

☐ If full hookup - put gloves on and dump black water - go inside and fill toilet with several gallons of water - dump black again to rinse tank. Close valve and add water and chemicals for when on the road

☐ Dump gray water and thoroughly rinse sewer hose, then store away

☐ Make sure both gray and black water valves are shut and cover is on securely.

DEPARTURE LIST (Cont'd)

☐ Remove sewer hose and rinse - pack away

☐ Check level of freshwater tank for on the road - add water if needed

☐ Unplug electric cord, cable/telephone connection and pack away

☐ Shut water off and disconnect water hose and pack away

☐ Pick up all trash and take to designated receptacles

☐ Shut off propane - check local and state laws.

☐ If towing a trailer - hitch up. When secure, remove wheel chocks and pack away check your hookup **twice**

☐ Check lights on tow vehicle and trailer

☐ Test brakes (brake system in tow vehicle)

☐ Always check bearings, tires and tow hookup at every stop

☐ Check all compartments - make sure all items are secure.

DEPARTURE LIST (Cont'd)

☐ Make sure all flammables such as lighter fluid, grille gas bottles, lamp lighter fluids are packed properly and securely.

☐ Check all lights - brakes, blinkers, headlights

☐ Check engine fluids, tire pressure, lug nuts

☐ Do the "WALK AROUND" - double check for any loose items that may have been missed.

☐ Make sure entry door is secure and locked.

☐ Check with your neighbors, Do they need any help with anything?   You may need help someday!

☐ Pull away from the campsite - get out and be sure the site is "**as clean or cleaner**" than when you arrived including fire place. Give your leftover firewood to your neighbors.

☐ Make sure all passengers and pets are secure

☐ If there are no full hookups - off to the dump station! Remember to rinse dump station area. WEAR GLOVES!!

☐ **Lastly,** make a point to keep in contact with family and friends when departing so they know all is well and you are safe.

DEPARTURE LIST

☐ _____

☐ _____

☐ _____

☐ _____

☐ _____

☐ _____

☐ _____

☐ _____

☐ _____

☐ _____

DEPARTURE FROM HOME BASE

- ☐ Stop mail delivery

- ☐ Stop newspaper delivery

- ☐ Set timers on lights

- ☐ Set thermostat (if leaving during winter months)

- ☐ Notify neighbors and family members

- ☐ Clean out refrigerator and any perishable foods

- ☐ Consider an alarm in your home

- ☐ Hire a housesitter

- ☐ Move all valuables (jewelry, cash, sentimental and irreplaceable items) to another location. Safety deposit box or another family members home if you're away for an extended period.

- ☐ _____

- ☐ _____

- ☐ _____

- ☐ _____

- ☐ _____

- ☐ _____

STORAGE LIST

I remember the first camper we purchased. It was a brand new Pop-Up with a shower and toilet! Oh my! It was huge. We were amazed at the amount of storage there was….. **with nothing in it.** Our first camping trip was a fishing trip in the early spring to a freshwater pond on Cape Cod, Massachusetts. There were 5 of us. 5 duffle bags, 5 sleeping bags, 5 pillows, 12 pairs of shoes & boots, 20 fishing rods, 4 tackle boxes, bait, 3 coolers, Oh yeah 2 dogs, dog bowls, dog beds, dog toys, towels, pots, pans, dishes, utensils, firewood, oh yeah **FOOD**, books, games, flashlights, toolkits….. I think you get the picture.

Most campers will soon find that any empty camper has a great deal of storage, it's when you start to **store** things in them, there's no storage!

We all can be guilty of bringing too much "stuff" and especially to much "food". Hopefully this storage list will give you a general list of necessary items. We all have our own personal things we bring along so add those to the end of this list. Remember, make room for necessary items so they can pack well while traveling. Packing too many items can only cause disorganization and can break easily if not packed carefully while traveling.

KITCHEN SUPPLIES

- [ ] Dishes
- [ ] Glasses
- [ ] Coffee Mugs
- [ ] Paper Plates
- [ ] Paper Cups
- [ ] Bowls
- [ ] Paper Toweling
- [ ] Napkins
- [ ] Coffee Maker
- [ ] Toaster
- [ ] Blender
- [ ] Pots and Pans
- [ ] Silverware
- [ ] Cooking Utensils
- [ ] Good Knives
- [ ] Scissors
- [ ] Trash Bags
- [ ] Aluminum Foil

- [ ] Plastic Wrap
- [ ] Plastic Bags
- [ ] Table Cloths
- [ ] Pet Bowls
- [ ] Spices
- [ ] Dish Soap
- [ ] Dish Rack
- [ ] Dish Clothes
- [ ] Pot Holders
- [ ] Can Opener
- [ ] Broom
- [ ] _____
- [ ] _____
- [ ] _____
- [ ] _____
- [ ] _____
- [ ] _____

BATHROOM SUPPLIES

- [ ] Towels
- [ ] Wash Clothes
- [ ] RV Toilet Paper
- [ ] Toilet Chemicals
- [ ] Cleaning Supplies
- [ ] Shampoo
- [ ] Soap (Ivory)
- [ ] Toothpaste and Toothbrushes
- [ ] Bug Spray
- [ ] Personal Items
- [ ] Hair Brushes
- [ ] Combs
- [ ] Hair Dryer
- [ ] Kleenex
- [ ] Deodorant
- [ ] Medicines/Thermometer
- [ ] FIRST AID KIT (always replenish)

- [ ] Sun Tan Lotion
- [ ] _____
- [ ] _____
- [ ] _____
- [ ] _____
- [ ] _____
- [ ] _____
- [ ] _____

MISCELLANOUS SUPPLIES

- [ ] Blankets
- [ ] Sleeping Bags
- [ ] Sheets
- [ ] Pillows
- [ ] Playing Cards
- [ ] Games
- [ ] CD's/DVD's
- [ ] **TOOL BOX**
- [ ] **Extra Light Bulbs**
- [ ] **Extra Fuses**
- [ ] Rope
- [ ] Camera
- [ ] Flash Lights
- [ ] Matches
- [ ] Books/Magazines
- [ ] Maps
- [ ] Citronella Candles
- [ ] Pads/Pens/Pencils
- [ ] Small Vacuum

- [ ] Fire Extinguisher
- [ ] Smoke Detector
- [ ] Carbon Monoxide Detector
- [ ] _____
- [ ] _____
- [ ] _____
- [ ] _____
- [ ] _____
- [ ] _____
- [ ] _____
- [ ] _____
- [ ] _____
- [ ] _____

OUTSIDE COMPARTMENT STORAGE

☐ Chairs   ☐ Levelers

☐ Tables   ☐ Propane Bottles

☐ Lanterns   ☐ Ant Cups

☐ Tools   ☐ Tarps

☐ Grilles   ☐ Trash Bags

☐ Outdoor Carpet   ☐ Pet Supplies

☐ Buckets   ☐ _____

☐ Shovels   ☐ _____

☐ Axe   ☐ _____

☐ Awning Pole   ☐ _____

☐ RV Extension Cord   ☐ _____

☐ Freshwater Hose   ☐ _____

☐ Sewer Hose   ☐ _____

☐ Gloves

☐ Firewood

☐ Fire starters

☐ RV Wash

☐ Extra Trash Bags

PET SUPPLIES

When your traveling with your pets, remember to make frequent stops to take them out and make sure fresh water is always available. Try to bring extra supplies such as leashes, collars and rope in case any are lost while on the road. It's also a good idea to find out about local veterinarians close to the campgrounds you are visiting in case of any emergencies.

- ☐ Current Medical Info - Rabies Cert.
- ☐ Pet Food
- ☐ Beds
- ☐ Crates
- ☐ Food Bowls
- ☐ Treats
- ☐ Leashes
- ☐ Runs
- ☐ Toys
- ☐ Fresh Water
- ☐ Towels (for rainy days)

- ☐ Dog Doo Bags
- ☐ Flea and Tick Repellant
- ☐ Brushes
- ☐ Medications
- ☐ Tweezers
- ☐ Hydrogen Peroxide
- ☐ Rubbing Alcohol
- ☐ Litter Boxes
- ☐ _____
- ☐ _____
- ☐ _____

SHOPPING LIST (BASICS)

- [ ] Paper goods
- [ ] Spring Water
- [ ] Bread
- [ ] Eggs
- [ ] Bacon
- [ ] Cereal
- [ ] Soda
- [ ] Butter
- [ ] Milk
- [ ] Coffee
- [ ] Cream
- [ ] Juice
- [ ] Sugar/Sweeteners

- [ ] Hamburgers/Hot Dogs
- [ ] Meats
- [ ] Pasta
- [ ] Condiments
- [ ] Spices
- [ ] Vegetables
- [ ] Fruit
- [ ] Cheese
- [ ] Snacks
- [ ] Ice

SHOPPING LIST

- [ ] _____
- [ ] _____
- [ ] _____
- [ ] _____
- [ ] _____
- [ ] _____
- [ ] _____
- [ ] _____
- [ ] _____
- [ ] _____
- [ ] _____
- [ ] _____
- [ ] _____
- [ ] _____
- [ ] _____

MAINTENANCE LIST

We have owned four different RV's… A Pop-Up, a 23' Travel Trailer, a 32' Class C Motor Home, and a 34' Class A Motor Home. One of the most important things that helped in the resale of each of our upgrades was the condition and maintenance of our previous RV. We sold the Travel Trailer to a private party and had records of all of the maintenance and warranty information.

After every camping trip, the trailer was cleaned inside and out. We owned it for 4 years and it looked like new. The first person who looked at it when we posted it in the want ad, bought it. Taking that extra hour to clean it after every trip and those extra few minutes to record information makes such a difference not only for resale value but also for your peace of mind as well.

We work too hard for our money these days, and if that money is being spent on an RV that we are going to enjoy for years and years, put your "non-work" time into taking care of your RV. Take pride in this possession. RV's can be expensive, and if you're making a payment every month on it or it's your retirement home, take care of it, educate yourself about every inch of this investment. You won't regret that extra time you put into knowing your RV. It may save you hours or even days of delay on an upcoming trip you've been planning.

Don't just plan your trip, plan your RV's maintenance schedule at the same time. They both go together!!

MAINTENANCE LIST

☐ Check Tire Pressure and Condition of Tires

☐ Check All Engine Fluids (Motorhome)

☐ Run the Generator at least once a month - maintain and
   keep oil changed.

☐ Inspect Batteries - clean terminals, check for corrosion

☐ Check under RV for leaks, loose items, dirt. Use WD40
   on moving parts on electric step. Dirt builds up on that
   frequently.

☐ Check roof for debris, cracks, leaks

☐ Maintain Exterior

    ☐ Wash Roof (remove sap, black streaks)

    ☐ Wash Exterior

    ☐ Wash Tires and Rims

    ☐ Clean Compartments including rims,
          interior doors

    ☐ Clean Electric Cord Compartment, cable/phone
      plug, water connection with damp cloth

    ☐ Wash Windows, Inspect Trim for Cracks and Leaks

MAINTENANCE LIST (Cont'd)

☐ Maintain Interior

    ☐ Clean all Appliances including inside Refrigerator

    ☐ Clean Counters/Tabletops

    ☐ Clean Sink, Toilet and Shower in Bath

    ☐ Clean inside Cabinets

    ☐ Polish Cabinets

    ☐ Clean Interior Windows Including Trim

    ☐ Clean Mirrors

    ☐ Vacuum Carpets

    ☐ Wash Floors

    ☐ Check Fire Extinguishers, Smoke Detectors & Carbon Monoxide Detectors

PART II - RV LOG

MAINTENANCE LOG

In Section I, we discussed general maintenance that you can complete and track. Section II is geared more towards recording general repairs you make or repairs that are completed at the dealership or manufacturer. Make sure to keep all of the receipts and documentation in a folder and note all the service that has been completed in this log.

Imagine your traveling across country and you breakdown. The situation is serious enough whereby your RV must be towed to a dealer. That dealer would certainly appreciate a complete record of maintenance. The dealer may even want to contact your dealer or manufacturer if the result of your breakdown is due to a problem with a previous repair.

Having organized, accurate maintenance and repair records can also assist in any warranty problems that may come up in the future. Having all of this information at your fingertips saves you "valuable vacation time" and money.

MAINTENANCE LOG (Cont'd)

<u>IMPORTANT:</u> Buy a Roadside Service Plan for "Your RV" <u>"Good Sam"</u> has an excellent plan that covers your RV and your vehicles at a very reasonable price. They also provide a wealth of information for RVer's.

We were at a campground in the summer of 2005 when a fellow camper next to us got a flat tire on his trailer on a bridge not far from the campground. Talk about a nightmare! He had to change the tire himself, on a very busy highway.

We had a copy of Good Sam's Magazine "Highways" in our RV and gave it to him. I told him he should join their roadside service program. He appreciated all the information, but that's what RV neighbors do.

MAINTENANCE LOG

Description _____

_____

Date _____

Materials _____Cost_____

Materials _____Cost_____

Materials _____Cost_____

Labor _____ Cost_____

Labor _____ Cost_____

Labor _____ Cost_____

Notes _____

_____

_____

_____

MAINTENANCE LOG

Description _____

_____

Date _____

Materials _____Cost_____

Materials _____Cost_____

Materials _____Cost_____

Labor _____ Cost_____

Labor _____ Cost_____

Labor _____ Cost_____

Notes _____

_____

_____

_____

MAINTENANCE LOG

Description _____

_____

Date _____

Materials _____Cost_____

Materials _____Cost_____

Materials _____Cost_____

Labor _____ Cost_____

Labor _____ Cost_____

Labor _____ Cost_____

Notes _____

_____

_____

_____

MAINTENANCE LOG

Description _____

_____

Date _____

Materials _____Cost_____

Materials _____Cost_____

Materials _____Cost_____

Labor _____ Cost_____

Labor _____ Cost_____

Labor _____ Cost_____

Notes _____

_____

_____

_____

MAINTENANCE LOG

Description _____

_____

Date _____

Materials _____Cost_____

Materials _____Cost_____

Materials _____Cost_____

Labor _____ Cost_____

Labor _____ Cost_____

Labor _____ Cost_____

Notes _____

_____

_____

_____

MAINTENANCE LOG

Description _____

_____

Date _____

Materials _____Cost_____

Materials _____Cost_____

Materials _____Cost_____

Labor _____ Cost_____

Labor _____ Cost_____

Labor _____ Cost_____

Notes _____

_____

_____

_____

MAINTENANCE LOG

Description _____

_____

Date _____

Materials _____Cost_____

Materials _____Cost_____

Materials _____Cost_____

Labor _____ Cost_____

Labor _____ Cost_____

Labor _____ Cost_____

Notes _____

_____

_____

_____

MAINTENANCE LOG

Description _____

_____

Date _____

Materials _____Cost_____

Materials _____Cost_____

Materials _____Cost_____

Labor _____ Cost_____

Labor _____ Cost_____

Labor _____ Cost_____

Notes _____

_____

_____

_____

MAINTENANCE LOG

Description _____

_____

Date _____

Materials _____Cost_____

Materials _____Cost_____

Materials _____Cost_____

Labor _____ Cost_____

Labor _____ Cost_____

Labor _____ Cost_____

Notes _____

_____

_____

_____

MAINTENANCE LOG

Description _____

_____

Date _____

Materials _____Cost_____

Materials _____Cost_____

Materials _____Cost_____

Labor _____ Cost_____

Labor _____ Cost_____

Labor _____ Cost_____

Notes _____

_____

_____

_____

MAINTENANCE LOG

Description _____

_____

Date _____

Materials _____Cost_____

Materials _____Cost_____

Materials _____Cost_____

Labor _____ Cost_____

Labor _____ Cost_____

Labor _____ Cost_____

Notes _____

_____

_____

_____

MAINTENANCE LOG

Description _____

_____

Date _____

Materials _____Cost_____

Materials _____Cost_____

Materials _____Cost_____

Labor _____ Cost_____

Labor _____ Cost_____

Labor _____ Cost_____

Notes _____

_____

_____

_____

CAMPGROUND LOG

Whenever we go on a camping trip, we always save the campground brochure especially if we liked the place. Then we find it balled up in the glove box of the truck, in the house or on the floor of the motor home with restaurant phone numbers on it and notes. We can never seem to keep the brochures all organized.

The **CAMPGROUND LOG** can keep all this information together. Note if it's a good or bad campground, rates, is it located near a main route, etc. It's also nice to have a record and look back at all of the places you've been to. Be sure to put the date you were there.

Ask other campers if they can recommend other campgrounds in the area or places to visit in that area. For example, if you're planning a coastal trip through New England, you may meet other campers that have already ventured that way and can recommend some great campgrounds and sites to see. Put those in the log.

Knowing the amenities of a campground can save you time. For example, if you are going to fish, find out if you can get your fishing license at the campground or do you have to get it in town, this will save time on your arrival. Even if you go to this campground every year, you tend to forget some important details.

CAMPGROUND LOG

Name _____

Arrival Date _____

Street Address _____

Mailing Address _____

City/State _____ Zip _____

Phone No. _____

Owners _____

Website address _____Email _____

Rates _____Season _____

Hookup Info   Full _____   W/E_____   Cable _____

Favorite site nos. _____   _____   _____

☐ Propane   ☐ RV Supplies   ☐ Web Access

CAMPGROUND LOG (cont'd)

Campground name (cont'd)_____

_____

Favorite sightseeing spots, restaurants: _____

_____

_____

Best Routes to use: _____

_____

Notes/Amenities:_____

_____

_____

_____

_____

CAMPGROUND LOG

Name _____

Arrival Date _____

Street Address _____

Mailing Address _____

City/State _____ Zip _____

Phone No. _____

Owners _____

Website address _____Email _____

Rates _____Season _____

Hookup Info Full _____   W/E_____   Cable _____

Favorite site nos. _____ _____ _____

☐ Propane   ☐ RV Supplies   ☐ Web Access

CAMPGROUND LOG (cont'd)

Campground name (cont'd)_____

_____

Favorite sightseeing spots, restaurants: _____

_____

_____

Best Routes to use: _____

_____

Notes/Amenities:_____

_____

_____

_____

_____

CAMPGROUND LOG

Name _____

Arrival Date _____

Street Address _____

Mailing Address _____

City/State _____ Zip _____

Phone No. _____

Owners _____

Website address _____Email _____

Rates _____Season _____

Hookup Info   Full _____   W/E_____   Cable _____

Favorite site nos. _____ _____ _____

☐ Propane   ☐ RV Supplies   ☐ Web Access

CAMPGROUND LOG (cont'd)

Campground name (cont'd)_____

_____

Favorite sightseeing spots, restaurants: _____

_____

_____

Best Routes to use: _____

_____

Notes/Amenities:_____

_____

_____

_____

_____

CAMPGROUND LOG D - F

Name _____

Arrival Date _____

Street Address _____

Mailing Address _____

City/State _____ Zip _____

Phone No. _____

Owners _____

Website address _____Email _____

Rates _____Season _____

Hookup Info   Full _____   W/E_____   Cable _____

Favorite site nos. _____ _____ _____

☐ Propane   ☐ RV Supplies   ☐ Web Access

CAMPGROUND LOG (cont'd)

Campground name (cont'd)_____

_____

Favorite sightseeing spots, restaurants: _____

_____

_____

Best Routes to use: _____

_____

Notes/Amenities:_____

_____

_____

_____

_____

_____

CAMPGROUND LOG

Name _____

Arrival Date _____

Street Address _____

Mailing Address _____

City/State _____ Zip _____

Phone No. _____

Owners _____

Website address _____Email _____

Rates _____Season _____

Hookup Info Full _____   W/E_____   Cable _____

Favorite site nos. _____ _____ _____

☐ Propane   ☐ RV Supplies   ☐ Web Access

CAMPGROUND LOG (cont'd)

Campground name (cont'd)_____

_____

Favorite sightseeing spots, restaurants: _____

_____

_____

Best Routes to use: _____

_____

Notes/Amenities:_____

_____

_____

_____

_____

_____

CAMPGROUND LOG

Name _____

Arrival Date _____

Street Address _____

Mailing Address _____

City/State _____ Zip _____

Phone No. _____

Owners _____

Website address _____Email _____

Rates _____Season _____

Hookup Info Full _____   W/E_____   Cable _____

Favorite site nos. _____ _____ _____

☐ Propane   ☐ RV Supplies   ☐ Web Access

CAMPGROUND LOG (cont'd)

Campground name (cont'd)_____

_____

Favorite sightseeing spots, restaurants: _____

_____

_____

Best Routes to use: _____

_____

Notes/Amenities:_____

_____

_____

_____

_____

_____

Name _____

Arrival Date _____

Street Address _____

Mailing Address _____

City/State _____ Zip _____

Phone No. _____

Owners _____

Website address _____Email _____

Rates _____Season _____

Hookup Info Full _____   W/E_____   Cable _____

Favorite site nos. _____ _____ _____

☐ Propane   ☐ RV Supplies   ☐ Web Access

CAMPGROUND LOG (cont'd)

Campground name (cont'd)_____

_____

Favorite sightseeing spots, restaurants: _____

_____

_____

Best Routes to use: _____

_____

Notes/Amenities:_____

_____

_____

_____

_____

_____

CAMPGROUND LOG

Name _____

Arrival Date _____

Street Address _____

Mailing Address _____

City/State _____ Zip _____

Phone No. _____

Owners _____

Website address _____Email _____

Rates _____Season _____

Hookup Info Full _____   W/E_____   Cable _____

Favorite site nos. _____ _____ _____

☐ Propane   ☐ RV Supplies   ☐ Web Access

CAMPGROUND LOG (cont'd)

Campground name (cont'd)_____

_____

Favorite sightseeing spots, restaurants: _____

_____

_____

Best Routes to use: _____

_____

Notes/Amenities:_____

_____

_____

_____

_____

_____

CAMPGROUND LOG

Name _____

Arrival Date _____

Street Address _____

Mailing Address _____

City/State _____ Zip _____

Phone No. _____

Owners _____

Website address _____Email _____

Rates _____Season _____

Hookup Info   Full _____   W/E_____   Cable _____

Favorite site nos. _____   _____   _____

☐ Propane   ☐ RV Supplies   ☐ Web Access

CAMPGROUND LOG

Name

Address

Street Address

City/State   zip

Phone #

Owners

Website/Page   Email

Rates   Season

Hookup Info: Full   W/E

Favorite site nos.

☐ Propane   ☐ RV Supplies   ☐ Web Access

CAMPGROUND LOG (cont'd)

Campground name (cont'd)_____

_____

Favorite sightseeing spots, restaurants: _____

_____

_____

Best Routes to use: _____

_____

Notes/Amenities:_____

_____

_____

_____

_____

_____

CAMPGROUND LOG

Name _____

Arrival Date _____

Street Address _____

Mailing Address _____

City/State _____ Zip _____

Phone No. _____

Owners _____

Website address _____Email _____

Rates _____Season _____

Hookup Info Full _____   W/E_____   Cable _____

Favorite site nos. _____ _____ _____

☐ Propane   ☐ RV Supplies   ☐ Web Access

CAMPGROUND LOG (cont'd)

Campground name (cont'd)_____

_____

Favorite sightseeing spots, restaurants: _____

_____

_____

Best Routes to use: _____

_____

Notes/Amenities:_____

_____

_____

_____

_____

_____

CAMPGROUND LOG

Name _____

Arrival Date _____

Street Address _____

Mailing Address _____

City/State _____ Zip _____

Phone No. _____

Owners _____

Website address _____Email _____

Rates _____Season _____

Hookup Info   Full _____   W/E_____   Cable _____

Favorite site nos. _____ _____ _____

☐ Propane   ☐ RV Supplies   ☐ Web Access

CAMPGROUND LOG

Street Address

City/State

Phone No.

Rate Includes

Hookup Info   WE   Elect

Favorite Sites

LP Propane   RV Supplies   Web Access

CAMPGROUND LOG (cont'd)

Campground name (cont'd)_____

_____

Favorite sightseeing spots, restaurants: _____

_____

_____

Best Routes to use: _____

_____

Notes/Amenities:_____

_____

_____

_____

_____

_____

CAMPGROUND FRIENDS

It's amazing how quickly you become friends with campers. We have camped along the Cape Cod Canal for the past 3 years now and have two special friends we see every year. It's the only time we see them and we pick up on the last sentence we were having last September when we arrive the next July.

We have formed lifetime friendships around campfires, at card games during a rainstorm, at a potluck supper, at a square dance, at a band concert, and on dog walks with our first morning cup of coffee. Keep in touch with your friends throughout the year with the **Campground Friends** section.

Name _____

Address _____

City/State _____Zip _____

Phone No. _____

Cell No. _____

Email Address _____

Other Information _____

Name _____

Address _____

City/State _____Zip _____

Phone No. _____

Cell No. _____

Email Address _____

Other Information _____

Name _____

Address _____

City/State _____Zip _____

Phone No. _____

Cell No. _____

Email Address _____

Other Information _____

Name _____

Address _____

City/State _____Zip _____

Phone No. _____

Cell No. _____

Email Address _____

Other Information _____

Name _____

Address _____

City/State _____Zip _____

Phone No. _____

Cell No. _____

Email Address _____

Other Information _____

Name _____

Address _____

City/State _____Zip _____

Phone No. _____

Cell No. _____

Email Address _____

Other Information _____

CAMPGROUND FRIENDS

D - F

Name _____

Address _____

City/State _____Zip _____

Phone No. _____

Cell No. _____

Email Address _____

Other Information _____

Name _____

Address _____

City/State _____Zip _____

Phone No. _____

Cell No. _____

Email Address _____

Other Information _____

Name _____

Address _____

City/State _____Zip _____

Phone No. _____

Cell No. _____

Email Address _____

Other Information _____

Name _____

Address _____

City/State _____Zip _____

Phone No. _____

Cell No. _____

Email Address _____

Other Information _____

CAMPGROUND FRIENDS

Name _____

Address _____

City/State _____Zip _____

Phone No. _____

Cell No. _____

Email Address _____

Other Information _____

Name _____

Address _____

City/State _____Zip _____

Phone No. _____

Cell No. _____

Email Address _____

Other Information _____

CAMPGROUND FRIENDS

Name
Address
City
Zip
Cell No.
Email Address
Other Information

Name
Address
City/State   Zip
Phone No.
Cell No.
Email Address
Other Information

Name _____

Address _____

City/State _____Zip _____

Phone No. _____

Cell No. _____

Email Address _____

Other Information _____

Name _____

Address _____

City/State _____Zip _____

Phone No. _____

Cell No. _____

Email Address _____

Other Information _____

CAMPGROUND FRIENDS

Name _____

Address _____

City/State _____Zip _____

Phone No. _____

Cell No. _____

Email Address _____

Other Information _____

Name _____

Address _____

City/State _____Zip _____

Phone No. _____

Cell No. _____

Email Address _____

Other Information _____

CAMPGROUND FRIENDS

Name
Address
City/State
Phone No.
Cell No.
Email Address
Other Information

Name
Address
City/State
Phone No.
Cell No.
Email Address
Other Information

Name _____

Address _____

City/State _____Zip _____

Phone No. _____

Cell No. _____

Email Address _____

Other Information _____

Name _____

Address _____

City/State _____Zip _____

Phone No. _____

Cell No. _____

Email Address _____

Other Information _____

Name _____

Address _____

City/State _____Zip _____

Phone No. _____

Cell No. _____

Email Address _____

Other Information _____

Name _____

Address _____

City/State _____Zip _____

Phone No. _____

Cell No. _____

Email Address _____

Other Information _____

CAMPGROUND FRIENDS P - R

Name _____

Address _____

City/State _____Zip _____

Phone No. _____

Cell No. _____

Email Address _____

Other Information _____

Name _____

Address _____

City/State _____Zip _____

Phone No. _____

Cell No. _____

Email Address _____

Other Information _____

CAMPGROUND FRIENDS

Name _____

Address _____

City/State _____ Zip _____

Phone No. _____

Cell No. _____

Email Address _____

Other Information _____

Name _____

Address _____

City/State _____ Zip _____

Phone No. _____

Cell No. _____

Email Address _____

Other Information _____

CAMPGROUND FRIENDS

Name

Address

Day/Tel.

Phone No.

Cell No.

Email Address

Other Information

Name

Address

Day/Tel.

Phone No.

Cell No.

Email Address

Other Information

Name _____

Address _____

City/State _____Zip _____

Phone No. _____

Cell No. _____

Email Address _____

Other Information _____

Name _____

Address _____

City/State _____Zip _____

Phone No. _____

Cell No. _____

Email Address _____

Other Information _____

RECIPES

A major part of camping is **eating**. Everything tastes and smells better when we cook over the campfire or even inside the RV.

When we sit down to eat breakfast we discuss what we will be having for lunch. When we eat lunch we discuss dinner. We meet campground neighbors in the late afternoon for cocktails and appetizers and have received many different recipes that we bring home and use throughout the year. You can keep track of all of these in the **Recipe** section.

RECIPES

Name _____

From _____

Ingredients

_____   _____

_____   _____

_____   _____

_____   _____

_____   _____

Instructions_____

_____

_____

_____

_____

_____

RECIPES

Name _____

From _____

Ingredients

_____   _____

_____   _____

_____   _____

_____   _____

_____   _____

Instructions_____

_____

_____

_____

_____

_____

RECIPES

Name _____

From _____

Ingredients

_____   _____

_____   _____

_____   _____

_____   _____

_____   _____

Instructions_____

_____

_____

_____

_____

_____

RECIPES

Name _____

From _____

Ingredients

_____ _____

_____ _____

_____ _____

_____ _____

_____ _____

Instructions_____

_____

_____

_____

_____

RECIPES

Name _____

From _____

Ingredients

_____   _____

_____   _____

_____   _____

_____   _____

_____   _____

Instructions_____

_____

_____

_____

_____

_____

RECIPES

Name _____

From _____

Ingredients

_____   _____

_____   _____

_____   _____

_____   _____

_____   _____

Instructions_____

_____

_____

_____

_____

_____

RECIPES

Name _____

From _____

Ingredients

_____   _____

_____   _____

_____   _____

_____   _____

_____   _____

Instructions_____

_____

_____

_____

_____

_____

RECIPES

Name _____

From _____

Ingredients

_____   _____

_____   _____

_____   _____

_____   _____

_____   _____

Instructions_____

_____

_____

_____

_____

_____

RECIPES

Name _____

From _____

Ingredients

_____   _____

_____   _____

_____   _____

_____   _____

_____   _____

Instructions_____

_____

_____

_____

_____

RECIPES

Name _____

From _____

Ingredients

_____   _____

_____   _____

_____   _____

_____   _____

_____   _____

Instructions_____

_____

_____

_____

_____

_____

RECIPES

Name _____

From _____

Ingredients

_____   _____

_____   _____

_____   _____

_____   _____

_____   _____

Instructions_____

_____

_____

_____

_____

RECIPES

Name _____

From _____

Ingredients

_____   _____

_____   _____

_____   _____

_____   _____

_____   _____

Instructions_____

_____

_____

_____

_____

_____

RECIPES

Name _____

From _____

Ingredients

_____   _____

_____   _____

_____   _____

_____   _____

_____   _____

Instructions_____

_____

_____

_____

_____

_____

RECIPES

Name _____

From _____

Ingredients

_____   _____

_____   _____

_____   _____

_____   _____

_____   _____

Instructions_____

_____

_____

_____

_____

_____

RECIPES

Name _____

From _____

Ingredients

_____   _____

_____   _____

_____   _____

_____   _____

_____   _____

Instructions_____

_____

_____

_____

_____

_____

IMPORTANT ADDRESSES/PHONE NUMBERS

Keep a record with you at all times of friends and family members at home. You never know when you might need to get in touch with someone back home. It's also nice to keep in touch with what's happening at home while you are on the road.

Name _____

Address _____

City/State_____Zip _____

Phone No. _____

Cell Phone _____

Email Address _____

Other Information _____

_____

Name _____

Address _____

City/State_____Zip _____

Phone No. _____

Cell Phone _____

Email Address _____

Other Information _____

_____

Name _____

Address _____

City/State_____Zip _____

Phone No. _____

Cell Phone _____

Email Address _____

Other Information _____

_____

Name _____

Address _____

City/State_____Zip _____

Phone No. _____

Cell Phone _____

Email Address _____

Other Information _____

_____

_____

Name

Address

City/State

Phone No.

Email Address

Other Information

Name

City/State   Zip

Phone No.

Cell Phone

Email Address

Other Information

Name _____

Address _____

City/State_____Zip _____

Phone No. _____

Cell Phone _____

Email Address _____

Other Information _____

_____

Name _____

Address _____

City/State_____Zip _____

Phone No. _____

Cell Phone _____

Email Address _____

Other Information _____

_____

_____

Name _____

Address _____

City/State_____Zip _____

Phone No. _____

Cell Phone _____

Email Address _____

Other Information _____

_____

Name _____

Address _____

City/State_____Zip _____

Phone No. _____

Cell Phone _____

Email Address _____

Other Information _____

_____

_____

Name _____

Address _____

City/State_____Zip _____

Phone No. _____

Cell Phone _____

Email Address _____

Other Information _____

_____

Name _____

Address _____

City/State_____Zip _____

Phone No. _____

Cell Phone _____

Email Address _____

Other Information _____

_____

_____

Name _____

Address _____

City/State_____Zip _____

Phone No. _____

Cell Phone _____

Email Address _____

Other Information _____

_____

Name _____

Address _____

City/State_____Zip _____

Phone No. _____

Cell Phone _____

Email Address _____

Other Information _____

_____

_____

Name

Address

City/State _____ Zip

Phone

Cell

Email Address

Other Information

Name

Address

City/State _____ Zip

Phone No.

Cell Phone

Email Address

Other Information

Name _____

Address _____

City/State_____Zip _____

Phone No. _____

Cell Phone _____

Email Address _____

Other Information _____

_____

Name _____

Address _____

City/State_____Zip _____

Phone No. _____

Cell Phone _____

Email Address _____

Other Information _____

_____

_____

Name _____

Address _____

City/State_____Zip _____

Phone No. _____

Cell Phone _____

Email Address _____

Other Information _____

_____

Name _____

Address _____

City/State_____Zip _____

Phone No. _____

Cell Phone _____

Email Address _____

Other Information _____

_____

_____

Name _____

Address _____

City/State_____Zip _____

Phone No. _____

Cell Phone _____

Email Address _____

Other Information _____

_____

Name _____

Address _____

City/State_____Zip _____

Phone No. _____

Cell Phone _____

Email Address _____

Other Information _____

_____

_____

Name _____

Address _____

City/State_____Zip _____

Phone No. _____

Cell Phone _____

Email Address _____

Other Information _____

_____

Name _____

Address _____

City/State_____Zip _____

Phone No. _____

Cell Phone _____

Email Address _____

Other Information _____

_____

_____

ADDRESSES/PHONE NUMBERS

Name
Address
City/State   Zip

Name
Address
City/State   Zip
Phone No.
Cell Phone
Email Address
Other information

Name _____

Address _____

City/State_____Zip _____

Phone No. _____

Cell Phone _____

Email Address _____

Other Information _____

_____

Name _____

Address _____

City/State_____Zip _____

Phone No. _____

Cell Phone _____

Email Address _____

Other Information _____

_____

_____

Name _____

Address _____

City/State_____Zip _____

Phone No. _____

Cell Phone _____

Email Address _____

Other Information _____

_____

Name _____

Address _____

City/State_____Zip _____

Phone No. _____

Cell Phone _____

Email Address _____

Other Information _____

_____

_____

Name
Address
City/State   Zip
Phone
Phone
Cell
Email Address

Name
Address
City/State   Zip
Phone No.
Cell Phone
Email Address
Other Information

Name _____

Address _____

City/State_____Zip _____

Phone No. _____

Cell Phone _____

Email Address _____

Other Information _____

_____

Name _____

Address _____

City/State_____Zip _____

Phone No. _____

Cell Phone _____

Email Address _____

Other Information _____

_____

_____

Name _____

Address _____

City/State_____Zip _____

Phone No. _____

Cell Phone _____

Email Address _____

Other Information _____

_____

Name _____

Address _____

City/State_____Zip _____

Phone No. _____

Cell Phone _____

Email Address _____

Other Information _____

_____

_____

Name _____

Address _____

City/State_____Zip _____

Phone No. _____

Cell Phone _____

Email Address _____

Other Information _____

_____

Name _____

Address _____

City/State_____Zip _____

Phone No. _____

Cell Phone _____

Email Address _____

Other Information _____

_____

_____

Name _____

Address _____

City/State_____Zip _____

Phone No. _____

Cell Phone _____

Email Address _____

Other Information _____

_____

Name _____

Address _____

City/State_____Zip _____

Phone No. _____

Cell Phone _____

Email Address _____

Other Information _____

_____

_____

Name

Address

City/State   Zip

Phone

Cell Phone

Email

Other Information

Name

Address

City/State   Zip

Phone No

Cell Phone

Email Address

Other Information

TRIP EXPENSE LOG

The **Trip Expense Log** is a great way to keep track of how much you are spending on each trip. Make a note of all of your expenses as you travel. At the end of your trip take a look at what your are spending and figure ways to cut down on your expenses. Instead of dining out for lunch, keep sandwiches ready in the RV and eat in a rest area or a scenic area. Buy certain items used all of the time in bulk from home like papergoods, bottled water, soda, etc and bring them along to save money on supplies. Watch your speed limits while traveling on the highway, to cut down on your gas expense.

The more money you save per trip the more trips you can take!

TRIP EXPENSE LOG

Trip Description _____

_____

Gas $ _____   Groceries $ _____

Gas $ _____   Groceries $ _____

Gas $ _____   Groceries $ _____

Gas $ _____   Groceries $ _____

Gas $ _____   Campground $ _____

Tolls $ _____   Campground $ _____

Tolls $ _____   Propane $ _____

Tolls $ _____   Propane $ _____

Tolls $ _____   Supplies $ _____

Dining $ _____   Supplies $ _____

Dining $ _____   Supplies $ _____

Dining $ _____   Misc. $ _____

Dining $ _____   Misc. $ _____

Dining $ _____   Misc. $ _____

Dining $ _____   TOTAL $ _____

TRIP EXPENSE LOG

Trip Description _____

_____

Gas $ _____   Groceries $ _____

Gas $ _____   Groceries $ _____

Gas $ _____   Groceries $ _____

Gas $ _____   Groceries $ _____

Gas $ _____   Campground $ _____

Tolls $ _____   Campground $ _____

Tolls $ _____   Propane $ _____

Tolls $ _____   Propane $ _____

Tolls $ _____   Supplies $ _____

Dining $ _____   Supplies $ _____

Dining $ _____   Supplies $ _____

Dining $ _____   Misc. $ _____

Dining $ _____   Misc. $ _____

Dining $ _____   Misc. $ _____

Dining $ _____   TOTAL $ _____

TRIP EXPENSE LOG

Trip Description _____

_____

Gas $ _____   Groceries $ _____

Gas $ _____   Groceries $ _____

Gas $ _____   Groceries $ _____

Gas $ _____   Groceries $ _____

Gas $ _____   Campground $ _____

Tolls $ _____   Campground $ _____

Tolls $ _____   Propane $ _____

Tolls $ _____   Propane $ _____

Tolls $ _____   Supplies $ _____

Dining $ _____   Supplies $ _____

Dining $ _____   Supplies $ _____

Dining $ _____   Misc. $ _____

Dining $ _____   Misc. $ _____

Dining $ _____   Misc. $ _____

Dining $ _____   TOTAL $ _____

TRIP EXPENSE LOG

Trip Description _____

_____

Gas $ _____   Groceries $ _____

Gas $ _____   Groceries $ _____

Gas $ _____   Groceries $ _____

Gas $ _____   Groceries $ _____

Gas $ _____   Campground $ _____

Tolls $ _____   Campground $ _____

Tolls $ _____   Propane $ _____

Tolls $ _____   Propane $ _____

Tolls $ _____   Supplies $ _____

Dining $ _____   Supplies $ _____

Dining $ _____   Supplies $ _____

Dining $ _____   Misc. $ _____

Dining $ _____   Misc. $ _____

Dining $ _____   Misc. $ _____

Dining $ _____   TOTAL $ _____

TRIP EXPENSE LOG

Trip Description _____

_____

Gas $ _____   Groceries $ _____

Gas $ _____   Groceries $ _____

Gas $ _____   Groceries $ _____

Gas $ _____   Groceries $ _____

Gas $ _____   Campground $ _____

Tolls $ _____   Campground $ _____

Tolls $ _____   Propane $ _____

Tolls $ _____   Propane $ _____

Tolls $ _____   Supplies $ _____

Dining $ _____   Supplies $ _____

Dining $ _____   Supplies $ _____

Dining $ _____   Misc. $ _____

Dining $ _____   Misc. $ _____

Dining $ _____   Misc. $ _____

Dining $ _____   TOTAL $ _____

TRIP EXPENSE LOG

Trip Description _____

_____

Gas $ _____   Groceries $ _____

Gas $ _____   Groceries $ _____

Gas $ _____   Groceries $ _____

Gas $ _____   Groceries $ _____

Gas $ _____   Campground $ _____

Tolls $ _____   Campground $ _____

Tolls $ _____   Propane $ _____

Tolls $ _____   Propane $ _____

Tolls $ _____   Supplies $ _____

Dining $ _____   Supplies $ _____

Dining $ _____   Supplies $ _____

Dining $ _____   Misc. $ _____

Dining $ _____   Misc. $ _____

Dining $ _____   Misc. $ _____

Dining $ _____   TOTAL $ _____

TRIP EXPENSE LOG

Trip Description _____

_____

Gas $ _____   Groceries $ _____

Gas $ _____   Groceries $ _____

Gas $ _____   Groceries $ _____

Gas $ _____   Groceries $ _____

Gas $ _____   Campground $ _____

Tolls $ _____   Campground $ _____

Tolls $ _____   Propane $ _____

Tolls $ _____   Propane $ _____

Tolls $ _____   Supplies $ _____

Dining $ _____   Supplies $ _____

Dining $ _____   Supplies $ _____

Dining $ _____   Misc. $ _____

Dining $ _____   Misc. $ _____

Dining $ _____   Misc. $ _____

Dining $ _____   TOTAL $ _____

TRIP EXPENSE LOG

Trip Description _____

_____

Gas $ _____   Groceries $ _____

Gas $ _____   Groceries $ _____

Gas $ _____   Groceries $ _____

Gas $ _____   Groceries $ _____

Gas $ _____   Campground $ _____

Tolls $ _____   Campground $ _____

Tolls $ _____   Propane $ _____

Tolls $ _____   Propane $ _____

Tolls $ _____   Supplies $ _____

Dining $ _____   Supplies $ _____

Dining $ _____   Supplies $ _____

Dining $ _____   Misc. $ _____

Dining $ _____   Misc. $ _____

Dining $ _____   Misc. $ _____

Dining $ _____   TOTAL $ _____

TRIP EXPENSE LOG

Trip Description _____

_____

Gas $ _____   Groceries $ _____

Gas $ _____   Groceries $ _____

Gas $ _____   Groceries $ _____

Gas $ _____   Groceries $ _____

Gas $ _____   Campground $ _____

Tolls $ _____   Campground $ _____

Tolls $ _____   Propane $ _____

Tolls $ _____   Propane $ _____

Tolls $ _____   Supplies $ _____

Dining $ _____   Supplies $ _____

Dining $ _____   Supplies $ _____

Dining $ _____   Misc. $ _____

Dining $ _____   Misc. $ _____

Dining $ _____   Misc. $ _____

Dining $ _____   TOTAL $ _____

TRIP EXPENSE LOG

Trip Description

Gas   Groceries $
Gas   Groceries $
Gas $ Groceries $
Gas   Groceries $
Gas $ Campfire
                             Campground
                             Propane $
                             Propane $
Tolls $ Supplies
Dining $
Dining $
Dining $ Misc $
Dining $ Misc $
Dining $ Misc $
Dining $ TOTAL $

TRIP EXPENSE LOG

Trip Description _____

_____

Gas $ _____   Groceries $ _____

Gas $ _____   Groceries $ _____

Gas $ _____   Groceries $ _____

Gas $ _____   Groceries $ _____

Gas $ _____   Campground $ _____

Tolls $ _____   Campground $ _____

Tolls $ _____   Propane $ _____

Tolls $ _____   Propane $ _____

Tolls $ _____   Supplies $ _____

Dining $ _____   Supplies $ _____

Dining $ _____   Supplies $ _____

Dining $ _____   Misc. $ _____

Dining $ _____   Misc. $ _____

Dining $ _____   Misc. $ _____

Dining $ _____   TOTAL $ _____

TRIP EXPENSE LOG

Trip Description _____

_____

Gas $ _____   Groceries $ _____

Gas $ _____   Groceries $ _____

Gas $ _____   Groceries $ _____

Gas $ _____   Groceries $ _____

Gas $ _____   Campground $ _____

Tolls $ _____   Campground $ _____

Tolls $ _____   Propane $ _____

Tolls $ _____   Propane $ _____

Tolls $ _____   Supplies $ _____

Dining $ _____   Supplies $ _____

Dining $ _____   Supplies $ _____

Dining $ _____   Misc. $ _____

Dining $ _____   Misc. $ _____

Dining $ _____   Misc. $ _____

Dining $ _____   TOTAL $ _____

NOTES

www.ingramcontent.com/pod-product-compliance
Lightning Source LLC
Chambersburg PA
CBHW080325270326
41927CB00014B/3098